TABLE OF CONTENTS

LIST OF TABLES

SUMMARY OF SOME MAJOR FINDINGS

*Law libraries are major users of E-books and legal publishing is one of the most fertile areas for E-book development.

*More than 41% of the libraries in the sample had a subscription to NetLibrary, including nearly 61% of the college libraries. About 78% of the librarians taking the survey had heard of NetLibrary.

*Almost 20% of the libraries in the sample had a subscription to an E-book service other than NetLibrary, or an E-book or site license deal for electronic content with a specific book publisher.

*About half of the libraries in the sample paid for E-books with funds taken from their traditional book budget. Nearly 60% of libraries in the sample believe that they could obtain special funding for E-books if the E-book industry develops quickly.

*Only a little more than 7% of the libraries in the sample say that their E-book collections have impacted their print book collection development plans.

*More than 22% of the libraries in the sample have E-book licenses that allow for simultaneous use of at least some titles in their E-book collection.

*Some of the more commonly used sites used by librarians for E-book downloading and viewing are E-books.com and Amazon.com.

*More than 13% of the libraries in the sample lend out to patrons some form of E-book reader specifically designed to access E-books (exlcuding CD-ROM/DVD readers).

*Almost 32% of the libraries in the sample have used the Franklin E-bookman

*More than 28% of the libraries in the sample have used a Palm Pilot to download E-books

*The Adobe Acrobat E-book reader was the most popular E-book reading software among the librarians in the sample

*Nearly 68% of the libraries in the sample offered access to public domain E-books.

*Almost 12% of the libraries in the sample have used Etext.Lib, a public domain E-book collection offered by the College of Virginia.

*Reference Literature was the subject category of E-books that attracted the most interest among library patrons, according to the librarians in the sample that used E-books.

*The list of specific publishers with which survey participants had E-book site licenses read pretty much like a Who's Who of legal publishing, including but not limited to The Bureau of National Affairs, Inc., Mathew Bender, Commerce Clearinghouse, West Group and others. A few reference publishers such as Gale were also on the list.

*The obstacle of individual books as "boundries" in the online search environment for E-books, the high cost of converting print to E-books, the lack of universal standards for E-books, the lack of comfort associated with on screen reading, and the competition for library workstations are all factors restraining E-books in the library environment.

Close to 17% of distance learning programs surveyed use E-books in their cirriculum, and distance learning students tend to be heavier spenders on educational materials than students in traditional classes.

In supplementary sample, about 34% of academic libraries offer an electronic reserve service to support training, course work, or other organizational objectives. Electronic course reserve services are among the primary users of E-books.

A survey by the NPD Group of online users (in May 2001) reported that 3% were "very likely to purchase E-books", 20% were "somewhat likely to purchase E-books", 45% were "not very likely to purchase E-books", and 32% were "not at all likely to purchase E-books." While it is not easy to interpret this data without knowing precisely the definition of E-book used in the survey, it raises the issue of "the glass half empty or half full". The survey data suggests that about a quarter of the online user population might at least make an initial E-book purchase and, while this does not seem like a very high figure, it is indeed high for an untested technology with little truly popular exposure. No major publisher has made truly major expenditures advertising E-books to the mass consumer market. E-books are only just beginning to make their impact on the most information-intensive sectors of the economy.

METHODOLOGY

The project started as a random sample of academic, public and special libraries, but the smaller academic libraries had few E-book deals and so, after a few interviews the frame of the study was changed to exclude the bottom half of academic libraries in terms of collection size. The medical, legal and corporate library market was randomly sampled without regard to collection size. The questionnaire appears in appendix 1.

Table #1: Constituents of First Sample

TYPE OF LIBRARY	Percentage of Sample
Academic	54.67
Special	41.33
Public	4.0

Table #2: Constituents of Special Libraries in First Sample

Type of Special Library	Percentage of Special Libraries in First Sample
Corporate	25.8
Legal	25.8
Medical	16.1
Other	32.3

Table #3: Constituents of Second Sample of Corporate Libraries

Industry Type	Percentage of Sample
Media/Publishing	8.3
MBA Program/Academic Business Library	10.4
Chemicals/Oil	10.4
Consulting	14.6
Pharmaceutical	12.5
Finance/Banking	12.5
Manufacturing	10.4
Other*	20.9

*Includes Defence, Telecommunications, Computing, Electric Power, Government /International Regulatory

Source: Data taken from survey of 48 corporate libraries from work in progress -- Corporate Library Benchmarks, 2002-03 Edition.

Note: Data for chapter 12 was taken from 2 other Primary Research Group reports: *The Survey of Academic Libraries, 2002 Edition* (sample of 66 academic libraries) and *The Survey of Distance and Cyber Learning Programs in Higher Education, 2002 Edition* (sample of 75 college distance learning programs). Data for tables #4 to #6 was taken from the Primary Research Group report *Digital Content Markets for Publishers*, which is based primarily on a survey of 300 U.S. publishers.

INTRODUCTION

The sample data suggests that E-book development will in certain key ways be somewhat similar to the development of other electronic publishing formats such as CD-ROM and web-accessed databases of newspaper and magazine articles. In the CD-Rom and web-accessed database industry, publishers were able to tap into and also create new markets for underutilized materials by collecting them into huge databases in electronic formats, offering search aids, thereby saving researchers time and money.

Just as these databases initially appealed largely to the most research intensive industries such as law and consulting, and research-oriented higher education, E-books have their greatest initial appeal with these audiences. Just as Cd-ROM and web-accessed databases spread quickly into the research intensive sectors of the daily life of students, journalists and others involved occasionally in research, E-books will spread through theirimpact on reference collections of public libraries and the electronic reserve section of academic libraries.

Growth rates over the past five years in the electronic content copyright information industry have largely been driven by an enormous conversion by major corporations from print to electronic information sources, led by information intensive industries such as consulting, law, pharmaceuticals, financial services, telecommunications and computing. These industries are now becoming relatively mature markets for growth in electronic databases of periodicals. However, they are just starting to acquire a taste for electronic books. It may be that the legal publishing industry, with its enormous appetitie for time saving search aids, will be the catalyst for other publishing industries to develop electronic books. At present, however, the potential in these industries is deeply limited by the "book as barrier".

Most E-book services and E-book licenses for individual publishers still tend to treat books as absolute discrete and separate units which, in some cases, can be individually searched, but are not "sliced" into topical units. One of the major reasons for the popularity of newspaper and magazine articles in databases is that the articles form small units that can be "called up" in through search terms. This extraordinary functionality enables end users to find relovent information much more easily than they are currently able to when using E-book databases.

Although many individual books can be searched using search terms in some services, the book forms an artificial boundry separating it from other elements of the E-book database. The equivalent in the world of newspaper and magazine dataabase publishing would be to allow searching only of specific issues of particular magazines. Imagine, for example, being able only to search the October 1999 edition of The Economist, and then having to search the November issue of The Economist, or the June 2000 issue of American Banker rather than being able to apply search terms to hundreds or even thousands of publications. Magazine and newspaper aggregators think of their digitized publications as parts of databases rather than as discrete unit essentially unrelated to one another. However, E-book vendors still treat their digital assets as discrete units, undermining a good part of their reference value.

It is useful for an end user in a company to be able to view a book online; he saves time by avoinding the bookstore or the library, and he is able to search the book more easily than he would a paper copy. however, these advantages are relatively minor since modern fulfillment and subscription services, as well as internet-based bookstores have reduced the time and cost burden of book acquisition. The time saved in being able to search a book electronically rather than consulting a print index is also very modest, unless the work is an encyclopedia, directory or other reference work that is fequently searched.

Consequently, E-books have not offered as many advantages to corporate researchers as electronic periodicals databases. In the academic market, this limitation also discourages the use of E-books. Imagine, for a moment, if a scholar preparing a paper on the author Bernard Malamud could scan the books of 100 leading American literature critics using the authors name or title of his books as search terms. The capacity to "pull down"specific chapters" and arrange them with those from other works would be an enormous time saver, a far greater time saver than current E-book technology generally permits.

However, since E-books cannot generally be searched in ways that ignore the "book as barrier" the most promising area for E-book development in academic settings has been in distance learning, reference services, and electronic course reserves. All of these areas share one characteristic: they all have populations that may need to consult a book frequently, simultaneously or both.

Generally, in the college-arena, supplementary educational materials rather than textbooks have been the more fruitful area for E-books. We do feel that in time -- perhaps 3-5 years -- it is possible that college textbook publishing could be dramatically impacted by digital editions and that as much as a third of this market could "go electronic" and be a huge catalyst for electronic sales. Once college students and faculty -- the second largest group of copyright information consumers after the information intensive corporations -- become accustomed to reading on a book access device -- they could serve as the sales base for the development of electronic editions. Currently, however, it is the supplementary and reference support areas that drive E-book development in academia.

In the electronic reserve, distance learning and reference markets, publishers undertandably fear that electronic access that allows simultaneous access could undermine print sales. Consequently, a solution must be found that enables libraries and colleges to "tap into" the enormous benefits of multiple access at low per unit costs that give publishers some combination of greater revenues and lower costs than they currently enjoy.

Where could these benefits come from and what are they?

The benefits are: no printing costs, no shipping costs, more exposure for print editions (Primary Research Group surveys of publishers have shown that most believe that electronic editions enhance print sales -- see later in this chapter). Another advantage: more readers, since simulateneous use of E-books will reduce "waiting time" to obtain the "book", thereby increasing readership. Indeed, studies show greatly increased use of titles when libraries offer them in digitized versions.

What are the advantages for libraries? Some are: lower storage and physical maintentance costs and no losses due to theft or loss. Most significantly, libraries will be better able to serve their cliente since key books will never be "checked out". This service depends on contract provisions that allow "simultaneous use".

The formula to any successful contractual relationship is mutual benefit. If publishers see E-books as a back door way to reduce revenues by depressing demand for key print books, especially when libraries need multiple copies, then publishers will naturally pull back. In the end, the E-book "contract" must be similar to the"contract" that makes databases of magazine and newspaper articles so useful to both information buyers and sellers. Buyers get enormous quantities of information at very low unit costs; sellers expoit and underused asset. What if book publishers refuse to develop E-books?

Won't competitors rush in with E-books that compete with the print books if those print book publishers refuse to develop E-books that might undercut their print sales? This has happened in some cases, expecially in the encyclopedia business, when CD-ROM editions of encyclopedias dramatically undercut the prices of existing print encylopedias, dramatically shrinking the print market. The major print publishers of encylopedias were slow to develop CD-ROM editions, or developed editions that were inferior to their print editions, so that these editions were not threatened by cheaper CD-ROM versions. They lost market share.

Another area of publishing slow to develop electronic editions was directory publishers and these publshers have seen some of their sales undercut by competitive web-based editions, and by internet search engines. The question is: will this happen in highe r education publishing if publishers refuse to supply E-books? Will these publishers lose out to electronic publishers that will in fact supply E-books with simulataneous access? Will the competitive dynamic of industry force publishers' hand, compel them to develop E-books or lose out to the electronic competition, as in the encyclopedia publishing business? The answer is: probably not.

In encylopedia and directory publishing, electronic editions, in CD-ROM or on the web, offer enormous functionality benefits over print editions. Directories and encyclopedias are not "read" so much as they are "searched", and the searching function takes up much more of the average end users time than in the use of other books, such as those typically on reserve for college courses or corporate distance learning programs. A new entrant with an electronic edition has a motive to make a large investment because the product developed can be a quantum leap over existing print products, and take away a large share of the market from print. In electronic course reserves, most books garner only a modest portion of their overall revenues from sales to libraries for course reserve. A competitive electronic edition would not be a quantum leap over the exisiting print edition, but only a significant improvement in one modest area. Professors are very unlikely to choose one book over another simply because one may offer an electronic edition suitable for electronic course reserve. Also, the cost structure of the publishers developing the electronic editions would not be significantly different from the cost structure of the publisher developing a print edition. The competitive dynamic does not lend itself to electronic editions undercutting the print editions, as it does in encylopedia and, to a lesser extent, directory publishing.

Since the competitive advantages of E-books for publishers are insufficient to allow E-book publishers to overtake print publishers in the library market, except in some highly specialized areas, print publishers will have to be reasured that they will make more money if they develop E-books than if they do not. Fears over digital piracy and negative impact on print sales have led book publishers to render their digital products less competitive than they might be if publishers could be reassured. The high profile failure of several major vendors of encryption technology in recent years has also not reassured the publishing community which, in reality, does not really want to pay very much for encryption technology.

The encryption technology market has generally been very difficult to supply profitably, and several companies offering encryption software or services have gone out of business in the past two years. Adobe appears to dominate the market, and most publishers appear to be using some form of Adobe technology, sometimes supplemented with Adobe "plug-ins" offered by other, generally small software companies

Publishers appear to have found other ways to deal with copyright problems, specifically four ways: 1) to tie digital purchases to the maintenance of print purchases, 2) to price digital products with the assumption of some fraud thus often raising digital prices above those of print prices, and 3) to restrict the quantity of information in digital format so that it does not undercut the need for the print product, 4) to make downloading, transferring, posting or printing so inconvenient or difficult that end users are discouraged.

The problem with these methods is that they all in some way make the product less desirable and hinder growth. Many consumers are paying a premium for electronic content when they should be paying less than the print price, not more, reflecting the lower printing and distribution costs, not to mention the increased ease of updating digital works.

In the end, publishers and libraries need to strike deals that deliver higher overall content profits to publishers, but with significant functionality and access gains for libraries. In areas in which E-books are most important now -- reference and professional literature, training, distance learning and course reserve -- publishers must ultimately trade lower per unit access costs for greater overall revenues through a combination of lower costs and increased usage, albeit at lower per unit cost.

A Primary Research Group survey of 300 American publishers of any of the following - books, directories, trade or consumer magazines, data or research reports, newsletters, newspapers and scholarly journals -- shows that publishers are already receiving close to ten percent of their PRINT orders from the web. This development encourages them to develop a web presence even when digital sales are not profitable.

Table#4: Mean & median percent of new print orders accounted for by orders through the web site for american publishers

	Mean Percent of new orders through the web site	Median Percent of New orders through the web site
All Publishers	9.73	2.0

Consequently, many publshers that do not currently have a web presence are considering developing one, as the following table shows.

Table #5: Percent of publishers that signed or are considering signing a deal with a content development firm to develop a "digital storefront" or other venue, broken out by annual revenues of publisher

Annual Sales Range ($)	% of Companies in Sample that have Signed Deal with firm to develop digital storefront or similar venue	% of Companies in the Sample Considering Such a Deal	% of Companies in the Sample Not Considering Such a Deal
Less than $3 million	17.8%	10%	73.2%
$3 million to $10 million	20.45%	25%	54.55%
$10+ million to $50 million	22.6%	26%	51.4%
$50+ million	50%	10%	40%

Of the companies in the sample with the lowest sales -- less than $3 million -- 17.8% had signed some kind of deal with an ecommerce, web development or content hosting firm to develop a digital storefront, website or other venue through which to sell the publisher's digital content, and another 10% were considering such a deal; in the $3 million to $10 million revenue range, 20.45% of the publishers had signed such deals, while another 25% were considering deals.

For organizations in the $10 to $50 million sales range, 22.6% had signed such deals, and other 26% were considering such deals. Among companies with sales in excess of $50 million, half had signed such a deal, and a further 10% was considering them.

About 65% of the publishers in the sample felt that their digital sales had little impact on their print sales, while 24% felt that it had helped print sales, and 5.5% felt that it had hurt print sales.   5.5% felt that digital publishing had helped for some publications but hurt for other publications in the publisher's product portfolio. Some companies did not answer this question, feeling that their digital efforts were so minimal or non-existent that the question did not apply to them. Also, keep in mind that many publishers set up their digital sales effort with the goal of making it not competitive with their print products.

Table #6: Impact of digital sales on print sales

Publishers View on Sales	% of Views
Digital sales had little impact on their print sales	65%
Digital sales hurt print sales	5.5%
Digital sales helped print sales	24%
Digital publishing had helped for some publications but hurt for other publications in the publisher's product portfolio.	5.5%

CHAPTER ONE: NETLIBRARY AND ITS SUCCESSOR

The NetLibrary Concept

NetLibrary was founded in 1998 as an ambitious attempt to develop and license E-books primarily, though not exclusively, to the library market, particularly the U.S. library market. Although the library market was its mainstay, NetLibrary also dabbled in print-on-demand books, downloaded books for the Palm Pilot, consumer-oriented E-books, and other markets. NetLibrary offered free access to public domain E-books, but charged a fee for materials with a current copyright. According to the company's press releases, the 'high use" areas of the NetLibrary collection are: Economics and Business, Medicine, Health, Wellness, Education, Technology, Engineering, and Computer Science.

Sale of NetLibrary to OCLC

The company was well financed, sales grew quickly, but very high levels of spending on marketing, technology and rights doomed the innovative company to the fate of many clever but extravagant internet startups: that of first casualty pioneer. NetLibrary's assets were purchased by the library cooperative OCLC in January 2002, reportedly for $10 million. OCLC has maintained the organization's brand and character, but integrated it into the OCLC.

An article in the Seybold Publishing Report (available on the world wide web) analyzes some of the reasons for NetLibrary's initial financial decline. Essentially, the company's story is similar to that of a great many startups in the information industry: it overestimated market potential, spent far too heavily on promotion and marketing, drifted into other markets which had no real synergy with its main market, and rang up relatively high data conversion costs. The company's general and administrative expenses alone exceeded revenues for one period in 2000.

According to the Seybold article, financial data about the Company's costs was made available through a prospectus launched by NetLibrary in August 2000. It showed marketing expenses for the first six months of 2000 of $12.6 million, $4.4 million on publisher rights and text conversion costs, $5.9 million on general and administrative expenses and $3.8 million on web operations and research & development. The company had $4.2 million in revenues in the same six -month period.

How Does the Netlibrary Concept Need To Be Adjusted?

NetLibrary allowed its patrons to "check out" a digital books in much the same way a patron takes a traditional book out of the library. Once a digital book was "checked out" by a patron, it could not be "checked out" by another patron from the same library, unless the library had paid a fee allowing multiple access for that title.

Although this feature reassured book publishers fearful that E-books would undercut print sales, it also negated one of the major advantages of electronic publishing -- the capacity for many users to simultaneously access materials.

For E-books to truly advance in the library market a solution must be found that reassures book publishers over copyright and impact on print sales issues, but also enables end users to enjoy some of the traditional advantages of electronic databases that they already enjoy in databases of newspapers and other periodicals. These databases thrive because they allow publishers to sell materials that otherwise would lie relatively dormant. Prior to the advent of online services and CD-ROM and other electronic databases, back issues of magazines and newspapers occasionally added value in reprints but were far less valuable than they are today. Publishers were able to sell access to these databases to researchers and libraries at very low unit costs, far lower than the sale prices of the publications on the news stand or through a print subscription. The sale of "back issues" did not in most cases undercut current sales, since most periodicals are "news-oriented"; their value is at least partially determined by their recentness.

Back issues of less "news-sensitive" publications, such as academic journals, were not generally sold through the large commercial online services or made available on CD-ROM or, currently, web-accessed databases. The value of their "back issues" does not decline as quickly over time. Consequently, licensing deals directly with publishers, or electronic sales "by the slice" have become the preferred mode of selling journal articles online.

Books do not decline in value with time as much as magazine and newspaper articles, and so the "database" approach of allowing multiple access to a very large database does not work well for books published in the past two years. However, for books that are older than this, this model might indeed be appropriate, with exceptions for frequently used titles that are not often updated. Many periodicals are "fit for the database" just a few weeks after publication; the gestation period for books is longer, but they have a gestation period. Book publishers have to be pried out of their "library check out model" for their backlists. Indeed, at least for backlisted titles that are two or more years old, publishers may be able to earn far more by harnessing the power of database distribution than by waiting for full price sales to libraries and research institutes. The selective use of very low prices and multiple access for older titles is one way to increase demand for those titles and increase their value.

Another model worth looking at for book publishers is the "Hollywood movie distribution model." Hollywood garners movie revenues from theatrical release, pay per view, video and DVD releases, cable television rental, national television rental, and local television rental. Each is timed so that revenue form one source can be "milked" before releasing the movie (often at a lower price point) to a new venue. First, the movie is released at the movie theater, at per person prices averaging about $8.00 to $9.00. Then, for some movies, it may enjoy a run on pay per view, for $4.00 to $6.00 for a showing, then a release on video or DVD for a dollar or two less and, finally, for showing on cable television, national television and local television. Each step down the ladder garners revenue at a different price point , but only minimally interferes with revenue from the source just "up the ladder." Book publishers in the consumer market already use this concept with the timed release of paperbacks at much lower price points than the hardcover price.

The leasing of older books at very low unit prices could also be used as an enticement for libraries to pay on a pay per view "check-out" type model for the most popular newer titles.

OCLC Plans

NetLibrary has been by far the most significant E-book venture, a pioneer that failed financially but may be revived by its new owner, OCLC. NetLibrary sold its assets to OCLC in January of 2002. Since then, OCLC has been trying to develop a new pricing model for the company. Its press reports suggest that the organization has interviewed hundreds of libraries and publishers in an effort to find a model that would meet publisher objections but also help make NetLibrary profitable.

It may be that OCLC will be better able to spread marketing, customer service and other expenses over an infrastructure already established to market to and service libraries. A trend has developed whereby established library-service providers such as Faxon and OCLC purchase upstart information services with novel technologies aimed at least partially at libraries. NetLibrary has already established impressive name recognition in the library market, and has an ample sales base on which to build. Recognition of the name "NetLibrary" by the libraries in the sample approached 80%, but was also highly imbalanced, with larger public and academic libraries virtually all recognizing the NetLibary name. Only slightly more than half of the librarians responding to the survey from the special libraries in the sample recognized the NetLibrary name.

More than 41.5% of the libraries in the sample had a subscription to NetLibrary, and the organization appears to be particularly strong in the college market, particularly among the larger colleges. Its penetration of the Special Library market appears much more limited.

Table #7: Percentage of libraries in the sample that have a current subscription to NetLibrary or its successor service

	Yes	No
All Libraries	41.56	58.44

Table #8: Percentage of libraries in the sample that have a current subscription to NetLibrary or its successor service, broken out by type of library

Type of Library	Yes	No
College Library	60.98	39.02
Special	12.90	87.10

Table #9: Percentage of College Libraries in the sample that have a current subscription to NetLibrary or its successor service, broken out by college enrollment

College Enrollment	Yes	No

Below 7,000	36.36	63.64
7,001- 13,000	70.59	29.41
Above 13,000	60.00	40.00

Table #10: Percentage of Libraries that have a current subscription to NetLibrary or its successor service, broken out for corporate and legal libraries

	Yes	No
Corporate	0.00	100.00
Legal	12.50	87.50

Table #11: Amount spent (in $) by the library for its NetLibrary subscription in the past year (current subscribers)

	Mean	Median	Minimum	Maximum
All Libraries	2510	1000	0	17000

Table #12: Amount spent (in $) by the library for its NetLibrary subscription in the past year, broken out by type of library

Type of Library	Mean	Median	Minimum	Maximum
College Library	2017	1100	0	9000
Special Library	1300	0	0	4000

The highest level of spending of any library in the sample on NetLibrary was a major city public library, which spent $17,000 annually.

Table #13: Amount spent (in $) by the library for its NetLibrary subscription in the past year, broken out by college enrollment

College Enrollment	Mean	Median	Minimum	Maximum
Below 7,000	1500	1500	0	3000
7,001-13,000	750	0	0	3000
Above 13,000	2067	1200	0	5000

Table #14: Percentage of libraries in the sample that have heard of the company name "NetLibrary"

	Yes	No
All Libraries	77.92	22.08

Table #15: Percentage of libraries in the sample that have heard of the company NetLibrary, broken out by type of library

Type of Library	Yes	No
College Library	95.12	4.88
Special	51.61	48.39

All three public libraries in the sample had heard of NetLibrary.

Table #16: Percentage of libraries in the sample that have heard of the company NetLibrary, broken out for corporate and legal libraries

Corporate	62.50	37.50
Legal	37.50	62.50

Table #17: Percentage of libraries in the sample that have heard of the company NetLibrary, broken out by college enrollment

College Enrollment	Yes	No
Below 7,000	100	0
7,001- 13,000	94.12	5.88
Above 13,000	90.00	10.00

CHAPTER TWO: SITE LICENSES FOR E-BOOKS FROM SERVICES OR SPECIFIC PUBLISHERS

Universe of Publishers with Site License Deals for Electronic Book Content

Nearly 20% of the libraries in the sample have some kind of a deal with an E-book vendor other than NetLibrary or a site license with a specific publisher. In the second sample of corporate and other business libraries, this figure increases to almost 33%.

In the universe of the academic and special libraries that comprise most of the sample, the data suggests a universe of about 2500 to 3500 libraries in the USA that have such site licenses, with about 20% of them academic libraries, and most of the rest accounted for by legal, medical and corporate libraries, especially legal libraries. Legal libraries were more than twice as likely as corporate libraries to have such site licenses and other special deals for digital books access. Nonetheless, levels of spending are largely modest, with median spending per library of $3,000.00 (US). Mean spending by special libraries was nearly twice that of college libraries even though after about 15% of the interviewing, only the larger college libraries were included in the sample frame. It is astounding that more than 85% of the legal libraries in the sample planned on additional E-book license purchases in the near future. Spending by the corporate libraries in the second sample, aimed at major corporations, was significantly higher.

Table #18: Percentage of libraries in the sample that have a subscription to any other E-book service or a deal with any specific publishers (including intranet licensing deals with book publishers)

	Yes	No
All Libraries	19.74	80.26

Table #19: Percentage of libraries in the sample that have a subscription to any other E-book service or a deal with any specific publishers (including intranet licensing deals with book publishers), broken out by type of library

Type of Library	Yes	No
College Library	14.63	85.37
Special	30.00	70.00

Table #20: Percentage of libraries in the sample that have a subscription to any other E-book service or a deal with any specific publishers (including intranet licensing deals with book publishers), broken out for corporate and legal libraries

	Yes	No
Corporate	25	75
Legal	62.50	37.50

None of the public libraries in the sample had a licensing deal with any specific book publisher.

Table #21: Percentage of libraries in the sample that have a subscription to any other E-book service or a deal with any specific publishers (including intranet licensing deals with book publishers), broken out by college enrollment

College Enrollment	Yes	No
Below 7,000	18.18	81.82
7,001- 13,000	17.65	82.35
Above 13,000	10.00	90.00

Table #22: Amount spent (in $) by the library for deals with specific publishers for electronic access to books in the past year

	Mean	Median	Minimum	Maximum
All Libraries	4050	3000	500	15000

Table #23: Amount spent (in $) by the library for deals with specific publishers for electronic access to books in the past year, broken out by type of library

Type of Library	Mean	Median	Minimum	Maximum
College Library	3000	3000	500	6000
Special Library	6500	3000	1000	15000

Table #24: Amount spent (in $) by the library for deals with specific publishers for electronic access to books in the past year, broken out by college enrollment

College Enrollment	Mean	Median	Minimum	Maximum
Below 7,000	2200	3000	500	4000
7,001-13,000	4000	3000	3000	6000
Above 13,000	4000	4000	4000	4000

Table #25: Estimated amount that libraries in the sample will spend on E-books in the coming year (including site licenses with book publishers)

	Mean	Median	Minimum	Maximum
All Libraries	5250	4000	500	15000

Note: the above Table # includes data only for those libraries in the sample that plan to spend anything at all on E-book deals with specific publishers, only approximately 23.4% of the libraries in the sample.

Table #26: Estimated amount that the library will spend on E-books in the coming year (including site licenses with book publishers), broken out by type of library

Type of Library	Mean	Median	Minimum	Maximum
Public Library	4500	4500	4000	5000
College Library	4609	4000	500	15000
Special Library	8250	7000	4000	15000

Table #27: Estimated amount that the library will spend on E-books in the coming year (including site licenses with book publishers), broken out by college enrollment

College Enrollment	Mean	Median	Minimum	Maximum
Below 7,000	2625	2500	500	5000
7,001-13,000	7000	7000	4000	10000
Above 13,000	5300	2600	1000	15000

Table #28: Percentage of libraries in the sample considering the purchase of an E-book or intranet license with any particular book publishers or service with which it currently does not have a deal, in the upcoming two years

	Yes	No
All Libraries	11.48	88.52

Table #29: Percentage of libraries in the sample considering the purchase of an E-book or intranet license with any particular book publishers or service with which it currently does not have a deal, in the upcoming two years, broken out by type of library

Type of Library	Yes	No
College Library	10.81	89.19
Special Library	10.53	89.47

None of the public libraries in the sample were interested in a deal with a specific publisher and most seemed more interested in dealing with aggregators. Most interest in the Special Library world is from law libraries but there is some nascent interest from medical libraries as well, but on a much lower level. Large academic libraries had some interest and medical school libraries might be a fruitful area for E-book development, but the broader medical market seems more doubtful at this time.

Table #30: Percentage of libraries in the sample considering the purchase of an E-book or intranet license with any particular book publishers or service with which it currently does not have a deal, in the upcoming two years, broken out by college enrollment

College Enrollment	Yes	No
Below 7,000	9.09	90.91
7,001- 13,000	14.29	85.71
Above 13,000	20.00	80.00

Table #31: Percentage of libraries in the sample considering the purchase of an E-book or intranet license with any particular book publishers or service with which it currently does not have a deal, in the upcoming two years, broken out for corporate and legal libraries

	Yes	No
Corporate	14.29	0
Legal	85.71	100

CHAPTER THREE: FUNDING E-BOOK COLLECTION DEVELOPMENT

About half of the libraries in the sample paid for their E-book licenses (or other types of E-book sales vehicle) from their traditional book budgets. However, the good news for publishers, and libraries, is that many librarians in the sample felt that they would be able to get special funding for E-books if the E-book market truly took off. This is a very good sign since special funding -- from foundations, alumni, library associations, wealthy donors, corporate departments that are heavy users of the library, government agencies, fund raising campaigns and the other myriad of sources for library funding -- has played a key role in library technology development over the last ten years. Librarians yearn to exploit their book collections with digital technology as they have with their periodicals archives.

The book -- however maligned in recent years in the pantheon of library assets -- still represents a key library asset, one which libraries are keen to exploit. E-books are often used by patrons to a far greater extent than traditional books in print collections. Indeed, one third of books in most research library collections are never checked out even once in their entire history in the library. Digitization of even a small number of titles can help librarians to help their patrons exploit a key resource. Some research studies have also shown that carrying a digital version of a title also helps to stimulate demand for the print version.

Table #32: E-books funding derived from traditional book budget

	Yes	No	Not Applicable
All Libraries	50.00	38.64	11.36

Table #33: E-books funding derived from traditional book budget, broken out by type of library

Type of Library	Yes	No	Not Applicable
College Library	55.56	40.74	3.70
Special Library	38.46	30.77	30.77

Table #34 E-books funding derived from traditional book budget, broken out college enrollment

College Enrollment	Yes	No	Not Applicable
Below 7,000	33.33	55.56	11.11
7,001- 13,000	75.00	25.00	0
Above 13,000	71.43	28.57	0

Table #35: Percentage of libraries that derive E-books funding from traditional book budget, broken out for corporate and legal libraries

	Yes	No	Not Applicable
Corporate	0	20.00	80.00
Legal	50.00	0	50.00

Table #36 Percentage of libraries in the sample that have received special funding to develop E-books

	Yes	No
All Libraries	15.79	84.21

Table #37: Percentage of libraries in the sample that have received special funding to develop E-books, broken out by type of library

Type of Library	Yes	No
Public Library	66.67	33.33
College Library	15.63	84.38
Special Library	9.52	90.48

Table #38: Percentage of libraries in the sample that have received special funding to develop E-books, broken out by college enrollment

College Enrollment	Yes	No
Below 7,000	20.00	80.00
7,001- 13,000	16.67	83.33
Above 13,000	14.29	85.71

Table #39: Percentage of libraries in the sample that have received special funding to develop E-books, broken out for corporate and legal libraries

	Yes	No
Corporate	12.50	87.50
Legal	0	100

Table #40: Percentage of libraries in the sample that may be able to obtain special funding for E-books in the future if the E-book market develops quickly

	Yes	No
All Libraries	58.93	41.07

Table #41: Percentage of libraries in the sample that may be able to obtain special funding in the future if the E-book market develops quickly, broken out by type of library

Type of Library	Yes	No
Public Library	66.67	33.33
College Library	60.61	39.39
Special Library	57.89	42.11

Note: Only 3 public libraries in the sample, all of which were from major population centers.

Table #42: Percentage of libraries in the sample that may be able to obtain special funding in the future if the E-book market develops quickly, broken out by college enrollment

College Enrollment	Yes	No
Below 7,000	40.00	60.00
7,001- 13,000	50.00	50.00
Above 13,000	87.50	12.50

Table #43: Percentage of libraries in the sample that may be able to obtain special funding in the future if the E-book market develops quickly, broken out for corporate and legal libraries

	Yes	No
Corporate	0	100
Legal	50.00	50.00

CHAPTER FOUR: LIBRARY PREFERENCES FOR VARIOUS ASPECTS AND FEATURES OF E-BOOKS

Most E-book users access their E-book collections from a remote server since this is generally considered easier and less expensive to do than to post a collection on an intranet. Major corporate and legal libraries sometimes prefer intranet posting, since they have tended to devote greater resources to developing data networks.

Large college libraries and corporate libraries and legal libraries had the most interest in books licensed for organizational intranets. Books accessed from internet sites on a subscription basis had a great deal of interest for corporate and legal libraries but also, to a lesser extent, for college libraries.

About 16% of the libraries in the sample have ordered print-on-demand books, and special libraries were more apt to have done so than college libraries. Legal and corporate libraries were the most likely to have ordered print on demand books. Close to 40% of the corporate libraries in the sample noted strong interest in the concept.

Public libraries and smaller college libraries had the greatest interest in books read through electronic reading devices. Larger college libraries and special libraries had generally lower levels of interest in this way of reading digital books.

For the most part, E-books for academic libraries have not yet had a significant impact on print book collection development policies and digital books still tend to still be viewed almost as novelty items, in striking contrast to digital databases of magazine and newspaper articles. Spending for these databases has had a significant impact on budgets for all other items, including print books.

Close to a quarter of the libraries with any kind of E-book collection or service have contract or other terms that allow for some form of multiple use. Special libraries in particular have negotiated these terms, perhaps reflecting the broader use of intranet licenses among this population.

Table #44: Library policies for storing E-book collections

	Housed on server or intranet	Housed on remote server	both
All Libraries	13.89	83.33	2.78

Table #45: Library policies for storing E-book collections, broken out by type of library

Type of Library	Housed on own server or intranet	Housed on remote server	both
College Library	19.23	80.77	0
Special Library	0	83.33	16.67

Table #46: Library policies for storing E-book collections, broken out by college enrollment

College Enrollment	Housed on server or intranet	Housed on remote server	Both
Below 7,000	0	100	0
7,001-13,000	30.77	69.23	0
Above 13,000	0	100	0

Table #47: Percentage of libraries in the sample that have ordered custom books or particular chapters or sections of books from a print-on-demand publisher

	Yes	No
All Libraries	15.71	84.29

Table #48: Percentage of libraries in the sample that have ordered custom books or particular chapters or sections of books from a print-on-demand publisher, broken out by type of library

Type of Library	Yes	No
College Library	12.82	87.18
Special Library	19.23	80.77

Table #49: Percentage of libraries in the sample that have ordered custom books or particular chapters or sections of books from a print-on-demand publisher, broken out by college enrollment

College Enrollment	Yes	No
Below 7,000	18.18	81.82
7,001- 13,000	12.50	87.50
Above 13,000	11.11	88.89

Table #50: Percentage of libraries in the sample that have ordered custom books or particular chapters or sections of books from a print-on-demand publisher, broken out for corporate and legal libraries

	Yes	No
Corporate	28.57	71.43
Legal	40.00	60.00

Table #51: Library interest Level in E-books downloaded from a web site as represented by self-selection in an interest category*

	1-Great Interest	2	3	4	5-No Interest
All Libraries	25.00	26.32	30.26	10.53	7.89

Key For Tables 51-70

1 = Great Interest   2 = Singinficant Interest   3 = Some Interest   4 = A Little Interest   5 = No interest

Table #52: Interest Level of libraries in E-books downloaded from a web site, as represented by self selection in an interest category broken out by type of library

Type of Library	1-Great Interest	2	3	4	5-No interest
Public Library	0	66.67	33.33	0	0
College Library	26.83	29.27	29.27	9.76	4.88
Special Library	25.81	19.35	29.03	12.90	12.90

Table #53: Interest level of libraries in E-books downloaded from a web site as represented by self selection in an interest category, broken out by college enrollment

College Enrollment	1-Great interest	2	3	4	5-No interest
Below 7,000	36.36	18.18	36.36	9.09	0
7,001-13,000	18.75	25.00	37.50	12.50	6.25
Above 13,000	20.00	60.00	10.00	10.00	0

Table #54: Interest level of libraries in E-books downloaded from a web site as represented by self selection in an interest category, broken out for corporate and legal libraries

	1-Great interest	2	3	4	5-No interest
Corporate	0	25.00	25.00	37.50	12.50
Legal	25.00	0	37.50	0	37.50

Table #55: Interest Level of Libraries in print on demand E-books as represented by self-selection in an interest category

	1-Great Interest	2	3	4	5-No Interest
All Libraries	14.47	21.05	19.74	25.00	19.74

Table #56: interest-level of libraries in print on demand E-books as represented by self-selection in an interest category, broken out by type of library

Type of Library	1-Great Interest	2	3	4	5-No Interest
Public Library	0	33.33	0	66.67	0
College Library	12.20	24.39	21.95	19.51	21.95
Special Library	19.35	12.90	19.35	29.03	19.35

Table #57: Interest level of libraries in print on demand E-books, broken out by college enrollment

College Enrollment	1-Great Interest	2	3	4	5-No interest
Below 7,000	9.09	54.55	18.18	9.09	9.09
7,001-13,000	12.50	18.75	25.00	25.00	18.75
Above 13,000	20.00	0	30.00	20.00	30.00

Table #58: Interest level of libraries in print on demand E-books, broken out for corporate and legal libraries

	-Great interest	2	3	4	5-No Interest
Corporate	37.50	0	37.50	12.50	12.50
Legal	12.50	0	12.50	62.50	12.50

Table #59: Interest Level of Libraries in books accessed through E-book reader

	1-Great Interest	2	3	4	5
All Libraries	17.11	11.84	18.42	26.32	26.32

Table #60: Interest Level of libraries in books accessed through E-book reader, broken out by type of library

Type of Library	1-Great Interest	2	3	4	5-No Interest
Public Library	66.67	0	33.33	0	0
College Library	17.07	9.76	21.95	31.71	19.51
Special Library	9.68	16.13	12.90	22.58	38.71

Table #61: Interest Level of libraries in books accessed through E-book reader, broken out by college enrollment

College Enrollment	1-Great Interest	2	3	4	5-No Interest
Below 7,000	27.27	9.09	9.09	36.36	18.18
7,000-13,000	25.00	18.75	18.75	25.00	12.50
Above 13,000	0	0	30.00	40.00	30.00

Table #62: Interest Level of libraries in books accessed through E-book reader, broken out for corporate and legal libraries

	1-Great Interest	2	3	4	5-No Interest
Corporate	12.50	0	0	50.00	37.50
Legal	0	25.00	25.00	12.50	37.50

Table #63: interest Level of Libraries in intranet licensed E-books

	1-Great Interest	2	3	4	5-No Interest
All Libraries	18.42	22.37	13.16	28.95	17.11

Table #64: Interest Level of Libraries in intranet licensed E-books, broken out by type of library

Type of Library	1-Great Interest	2	3	4	5-No interest
Public Library	0	0	33.33	33.33	33.33
College Library	21.95	21.95	12.20	31.71	12.20
Special Library	16.13	25.81	12.90	25.81	19.35

Table #65: Interest Level of Libraries in intranet licensed E-books, broken out by college enrollment

College Enrollment	1-No Interest	2	3	4	5-Great Interest
Below 7,000	9.09	18.18	27.27	36.36	9.09
7,000-13,000	18.75	25.00	12.50	37.50	6.25
Above 13,000	40.00	10.00	0	20.00	30.00

Table #66: Interest Level of Libraries in intranet licensed E-books, broken out for corporate and legal libraries

	1-No Interest	2	3	4	5-Great interest
Corporate	25.00	37.50	12.50	0	25.00
Legal	12.50	50.00	12.50	12.50	12.50

Table #67: Interest Level of Libraries in E-books accessed from a web site but not downloaded

	1-Great interest	2	3	4	5-No interest
All Libraries	25.00	19.74	19.74	9.21	26.32

Table #68: Interest Level of libraries in E-books accessed from a web site but not downloaded, broken out by type of library

Type of Library	1-Great interest	2	3	4	5-No interest
Public Library	33.33	0	0	0	66.67
College Library	21.95	17.07	17.07	7.32	36.59
Special Library	29.03	25.81	25.81	9.68	9.68

Table #69: Interest Level of libraries in E-books accessed from a web site but not downloaded, broken out by college enrollment

College Enrollment	1-Great interest	2	3	4	5-No interest
Below 7,000	18.18	0	9.09	9.09	63.64
7,000-13,000	25.00	18.75	12.50	0	43.75
Above 13,000	20.00	30.00	30.00	10.00	10.00

Table #70: Interest Level of libraries in E-books accessed from a web site but not downloaded, broken out for corporate and legal libraries

	1-Great interest	2	3	4	5-No interest
Corporate	25.00	37.50	25.00	0	12.50
Legal	50.00	25.00	12.50	12.50	0

Table #71: Percentage of libraries in the sample indicating that E-book collection has impacted print book collection development in particular ways

	Substituted E-books for print books	E-books stimulated demand for print books	Had no real impact
All Libraries	7.14	4.76	88.10

Table #72: Percentage of libraries in the sample indicating that E-book collection has impacted print book collection development In particular ways, broken out by type of library

Type of Library	Substituted E-books for print books	E-books stimulated demand for print books	Had no real impact
Public Library	33.33	0	66.67
College Library	3.45	3.45	93.10
Special Library	11.11	11.11	77.78

Table #73: Percentage of libraries in the sample indicating that E-book collection has impacted print book collection development in particular ways, broken out by college enrollment

College Enrollment	Substituted E-books for print books	E-books stimulated demand for print books	Had no real impact on print collection
Below 7,000	0	0	100
7,001-13,000	8.33	8.00	83.33
Above 13,000	0	0	100

Table #74: Percent of E-book collections allowing specific downloading and printing policies

	Allows Download of a digital copy	Allows Print out complete version	Print out selected pages only	Read only
All Libraries	5.13	2.56	79.49	12.82

Table #75: Percent of E-book collections allowing specific downloading and printing policies, broken out by type of library

Type of Library	Allows download of a digital copy	Allows print out complete version	Print out selected pages	Read only
Public Library	0	0	100	0
College Library	6.90	3.45	79.31	10.34
Special Library	0	0	66.67	33.33

Table #76: E-book collection downloading and printing policy, broken out by college enrollment

College Enrollment	Allows download of a digital copy	Allows print out complete version	Print out selected pages	Read only
Below 7,000	0	11.11	77.78	11.11
7,001-13,000	8.33	0	75.00	16.67
Above 13,000	20.00	0	80.00	0

Table #77: Percentage of libraries in the sample with E-book collections that formally monitor and have statistical data on the use of E-books

	Yes	No
All Libraries	36.36	63.64

Table #78: Percentage of libraries in the sample with E-book collections that formally monitor and have statistical data on the use of E-books, broken out by type of library

Type of Library	Yes	No
College Library	36.36	63.64
Special Library	27.78	72.22

Table #79: Percentage of libraries in the sample that formally monitor and have statistical data on the use of E-books, broken out by college enrollment

College Enrollment	Yes	No
Below 7,000	30.00	70.00
7,001- 13,000	46.15	53.85
Above 13,000	28.57	71.43

Table #80: Percentage of libraries in the sample that formally monitor and have statistical data on the use of E-books, broken out for corporate and legal libraries

	Yes	No
Corporate	0	100
Legal	25.00	75.00

Table #81: Percentage of libraries in the sample that have E-book licenses that allow for any simultaneous use of titles in the E-book collection

	Yes	No
All Libraries	22.50	77.50

Table #82: Percentage of libraries in the sample that have E-book licenses that allow for any simultaneous use of titles in the E-book collection, broken out by type of library

Type of Library	Yes	No
Public Library	0	100
College Library	22.22	77.78
Special Library	33.33	66.67

Table #83: Percentage of libraries in the sample that have E-book licenses that allow for any simultaneous use of titles in the E-book collection, broken out by college enrollment

College Enrollment	Yes	No
Below 7,000	25.00	75.00
7,001- 13,000	16.67	83.33
Above 13,000	0	100

CHAPTER FIVE: USE OF SPECIFIC E-BOOK SITES, SOFTWARE OR DEVICES

The following section offers data on the use of specific eb00k sites, software or devices, preceded by a brief overview of the product about which we asked.   Some of these products were:

Audiobooks.Com -- This is a favorite site for audiobook sales on the web. The site will soon allow direct download of audiobooks to personal computers and other access devices. Since most users of audiobooks are accustomed to cassettes and CD's, we feel it will be a natural transition for audiobook users to download audiobooks from the web. Currently, a relatively large percentage of the libraries interviewed for this study have used the audiobooks site.

Books 24x7 is a subscription driven service that offers subscriber access to content in exchange for a monthly fee based on the number of viewers allowed to access the content. The company specializes in technical and professional literature and publishers focusing on professional needs, such as John Wiley and MIT Press, are key contributors. The service offers access to a broad range of content at relatively low prices, and is somewhat similar in style to the vast databases of information offered through databases of newspaper and magazine articles. In this sense, its approach is different from that taken by many E-book vendors, who see E-books as "individual books for sale" rather than as segments of vast databases. Publishers may control their exposure on books 24X7 by testing out new books through the service, limiting the number of books on the service, or introducing them after print exposure -- preserving print sales.

E-books.Com -- is an Australian company that offers downloads of entire books, or parts of books, in Adobe format, direct from its website. The company is initially targeting business and reference users, but it has offerings in many different product areas. The company's web site is fun to browse and its E-book prices are lower than those of print publishers, but its title selection is significantly limited. The company might benefit from offering traditional print books form its site as well as E-books, since many competitors will, at least initially, be offering both.

Teachnow -- offers low cost educational materials for K-12 educators, with an emphasis on the K-4 market.

Lightning Source: Lightning Source is a print-on-demand service owned by Ingram, a major book distributor. The company is best known as a supplier of print-on-demand books, but it is reportedly branching out into the direct supply of E-books. The company's web site notes that is has supplied more than "3 million" print on demand books. For more information, visit the website at http://www.lightningsource.com . Industry sources suggest that the company was produced print on demand books for more than 1000 publishers.

Amazon.Com -- Amazon is positioning itself as a gateway to the E-book world by forging a series of alliances with key E-book players. In 2001, Amazon reached an arrangement with Adobe to distribute for sale E-books in the Adobe format. The company also has E-book alliances with Lightning Source, Microsoft, and other major players.

Palm Inc.   The owner/marketer of Palm Pilot noted in a Jan 2002 press release that it had sold 180,000 E-books in 2001, a 40% increase over year 2000 sales. The company notes that it acquires more than 1000 new E-book customers a week, and that is has 3,500 titles available for download. The company's top 10 fiction and non-fiction best sellers for 2001 are reproduced below:

Palm Digital Media Top 10 Best-selling Fiction E-books for 2001
   1. "Dreamcatcher" by Stephen King (Simon & Schuster)
   2. "Timeline" by Michael Crichton (Random House)
   3. "Riding the Bullet" by Stephen King (Simon & Schuster)
   4. "The Talisman" by Stephen King and Peter Straub (Random House)
   5. "Black House" by Stephen King and Peter Straub (Random House)
   6. "The Hades Factor" by Robert Ludlum and Gayle Lynds (St. Martin's Press)
   7. "Digital Fortress" by Dan Brown (St. Martin's Press)
   8. "Star Wars: Darth Maul: Saboteur" by James Luceno (Random House)
   9. "K-PAX" by Gene Brewer (St. Martin's Press)
   10. "The Jupiter Theft" by Donald Moffett (e-reads)

Palm Digital Media Top 10 Best-selling Non-fiction E-books for 2001
   1. "The Procrastinator's Handbook" by Rita Emmett, (Walker and Company)
   2. "Jack: Straight From the Gut" by Jack Welch and John Byrne (AOL Time

Warner Book Group)
   3. "The 7 Habits of Highly Effective People" by Stephen R. Covey
      (Franklin Covey)
   4. "Surfing the Edge of Chaos" by Pascale, Millemann and Gioja (Crown
      Publishers)
   5. "Get Anyone To Do Anything and Never Feel Powerless Again" by David
J.
      Lieberman (St. Martin's Press)
   6. "Useless Sexual Trivia" by Shane Mooney (Fireside)
   7. "Dave Barry Is Not Taking This Sitting Down" by Dave Barry (Crown
      Publishers)
   8. "52 Saturday Nights" by Joan Elizabeth Lloyd (AOL Time Warner Book
      Group)
   9. "Now and Forever, Let's Make Love" by Joan Elizabeth Lloyd (AOL Time
      Warner Book Group)
   10. "The Vagina Monologues" by Eve Ensler (Villard)

Barnesandnoble.Com   Barnesand Nobl.com purchased FATBRAIN in
2001.   Fatbrain originally started as an E-book publisher but later shifted
its focus to become a developer of "intranet bookstores" through which
corporations could purchase E-books and traditional books from their own
intranets. BarnesandNoble reportedly paid $64 million for the company.
The logic of the Fatbrain intranet library concept was to allow companies
to reduce their investment in libraries, archives and other information
depositories by enabling them to order materials "as needed" in both
paper and digital formats, directly from the company intranet. Many
companies in high tech industries such as telecommunications and
computing were particularly interested in this concept although some
main line industrials such as Ford also use Fatbrain.

BarnesandNoble.com streamlined Fatbrain and reduced the scope of the
enterprise while retaining the essentials of its vision. According to press
reports Fatbrain sales fell 25% in 2001, perhaps reflecting Barnes and
Nobles more focused plans for the organization, as well as the geneal
weakness of the corporate book market. Competition between traditional
book procurement companies and cyberspace oriented firms such as
Fatbrain, Rowe, Amazon and others, has hieghtened competition in the
book distribution business and probably has reduced rates of return as
well.

Pocketmanager.Com offers predominantly business and professional books, aimed largely at corporate executives and other high- income professionals.

The Franklin E-bookman The Franklin E-bookman was originally introduced as a device that could download E-books from the internet in 1999. The Company originally made its name in the portable electronic device market, particularly its electronic reference works such as dictionaries, thesauri and encyclopedias.

The range of titles available for the E-bookman includes audiobooks (which the E-bookman can read back" to the end user", and several thousand business titles in a range of languages.

Franklin also offers a library of several thousand public domain works, mostly classics, for free download.. The Franklin E-bookman can also download and view files in dos text and html, opening it to numerous digital libraries offered over the internet.

The strategy, as with most E-book publishers and ventures, is to increase the usefulness of the machine by making it a compatible as possible with other E-book formats.

Table #84: Percentage of libraries in the sample that have used E-books.com for E-book viewing or downloading

	Yes	No
All Libraries	50.00	50.00

Table #85: Percentage of libraries in the sample that have used E-books.com for E-book viewing or downloading, broken out by type of library

Type of Library	Yes	No
Public Library	100	0
College Library	38.46	61.54
Special Library	57.14	42.86

Table #86: Percentage of libraries in the sample that have used E-books.com for E-book viewing or downloading, broken out by college enrollment

College Enrollment	Yes	No
Below 7,000	28.57	71.43
7,001- 13,000	66.67	33.33
Above 13,000	0	100

Table #87: Percentage of libraries in the sample that have used E-books.com for E-book viewing or downloading, broken out for corporate and legal libraries

	Yes	No
Corporate	0	100
Legal	0	100

Table #88: Percentage of libraries in the sample that have used Teach now for E-book viewing or downloading

	Yes	No
All Libraries	0	100.00

Table #89: Percentage of libraries in the sample that have used Teach now for E-book viewing or downloading, broken out by type of library

Type of Library	Yes	No
College Library	0	100
Special Library	0	100

Table #90: Percentage of libraries in the sample that have used Teach Now for E-book viewing or downloading, broken out by college enrollment

College Enrollment	Yes	No
Below 7,000	0	100
7,001- 13,000	0	100
Above 13,000	0	100

Table #91: Percentage of libraries in the sample that have used Teach Now for E-book viewing or downloading, broken out for corporate and legal libraries

	Yes	No
Corporate	0	100
Legal	0	100

Table #92: Percentage of libraries in the sample that have used Audiobooks.com for E-book viewing or downloading

	Yes	No
All Libraries	27.27	72.73

Table #93: Percentage of libraries in the sample that have used Audiobooks.com for E-book viewing or downloading, broken out by type of library

Type of Library	Yes	No
College Library	23.08	76.92
Special Library	28.57	71.43

Table #94: Percentage of libraries in the sample that have used Audiobooks.com for E-book viewing or downloading, broken out for corporate and legal libraries

	Yes	No
Corporate	0	100
Legal	0	100

Table #95: Percentage of libraries in the sample that have used Audiobooks.com for E-book viewing or downloading, broken out by college enrollment

College Enrollment	Yes	No
Below 7,000	0	100
7,001- 13,000	66.67	33.33
Above 13,000	0	100

Table #96: Percentage of libraries in the sample that have used Lightning Source for E-book viewing or downloading

	Yes	No
All Libraries	0	100.00

Table #97: Percentage of libraries in the sample that have used Amazon.com for E-book viewing or downloading

	Yes	No
All Libraries	81.82	18.18

Table #98: Percentage of libraries in the sample that have used Amazon.com for E-book viewing or downloading, broken out by type of library

Type of Library	Yes	No
College Library	84.62	15.38
Special Library	85.71	14.29

Table #99: Percentage of libraries in the sample that have used Amazon.com for E-book viewing or downloading, broken out by college enrollment

College Enrollment	Yes	No
Below 7,000	71.43	28.57
7,001- 13,000	100	0
Above 13,000	100	0

Table #100: Percentage of libraries in the sample that have used Amazon.com for E-book viewing or downloading, broken out for corporate and legal libraries

	Yes	No
Corporate	0	100
Legal	100	0

Table #101: Percentage of libraries in the sample that have used Overdrive.com for E-book viewing or downloading

	Yes	No
All Libraries	0	100.00

Table #102: Percentage of libraries in the sample that have used Overdrive.com for E-book viewing or downloading, broken out for corporate and legal libraries

	Yes	No
Corporate	0	100
Legal	0	100

Table #103: Percentage of libraries in the sample that have used 1st Books.com for E-book viewing or downloading

	Yes	No
All Libraries	4.55	95.45

Table #104: Percentage of libraries in the sample that have used 1st Books.com for E-book viewing or downloading, broken out by type of library

Type of Library	Yes	No
College Library	0	100
Special Library	14.29	85.71

Table #105: Percentage of libraries in the sample that have used 1st Books.com for E-book viewing or downloading, broken out by college enrollment

College Enrollment	Yes	No
Below 7,000	0	100
7,001- 13,000	0	100
Above 13,000	0	100

Table #106: Percentage of libraries in the sample that have used 1ˢᵗ Books.com for E-book viewing or downloading, broken out for corporate and legal libraries

	Yes	No
Corporate	0	100
Legal	33.33	66.67

Table #107: Percentage of libraries in the sample that have used 00H00.com for E-book viewing or downloading

	Yes	No
All Libraries	0	100.00

Table #108: Percentage of libraries in the sample that have used Ebrary for E-book viewing or downloading

	Yes	No
All Libraries	0	100

Table #109: Percentage of libraries in the sample that have used Mightywords.com (fatbrain) for E-book viewing or downloading

	Yes	No
All Libraries	0	100

Table #110: Percentage of libraries in the sample that have used Librius.com for E-book viewing or downloading

	Yes	No
All Libraries	0	100

Table #111: Percentage of libraries in the sample that have used Books 24x7 for E-book viewing or downloading

	Yes	No
All Libraries	4.55	95.45

Table #112: Percentage of libraries in the sample that have used Books 24x7 for E-book viewing or downloading, broken out by type of library

Type of Library	Yes	No
College Library	7.69	92.31
Special Library	0	100

Table #113: Percentage of libraries in the sample that have used Books 24x7 for E-book viewing or downloading, broken out by college enrollment

College Enrollment	Yes	No
Below 7,000	14.29	85.71
7,001- 13,000	0	100
Above 13,000	0	100

Table #114: Percentage of libraries in the sample that have used Books 24x7 for E-book viewing or downloading, broken out for corporate and legal libraries

	Yes	No
Corporate	0	100
Legal	0	100

Table #115: Percentage of libraries in the sample that have used Ibooks.com for E-book viewing or downloading

	Yes	No
All Libraries	0	100

Table #116: Percentage of libraries in the sample that have used Adobe E-bookstore for E-book viewing or downloading

	Yes	No
All Libraries	0	100

Table #117: Percentage of libraries in the sample that have used BarnesandNoble.com for E-book viewing or downloading

	Yes	No
All Libraries	4.55	95.45

Table #118: Percentage of libraries in the sample that have used BarnesandNoble.com for E-book viewing or downloading, broken out by type of library

Type of Library	Yes	No
College Library	7.69	92.31
Special Library	0	100

Table #119: Percentage of libraries in the sample that have used BarnesandNoble.com for E-book viewing or downloading, broken out by college enrollment

College Enrollment	Yes	No
Below 7,000	0	100
7,001- 13,000	0	100
Above 13,000	100	0

Table #120: Percentage of libraries in the sample that have used BarnesandNoble.com for E-book viewing or downloading, broken out for corporate and legal libraries

	Yes	No
Corporate	0	100
Legal	0	100

Table #121: Percentage of libraries in the sample that have used Pocketmanager.com for E-book viewing or downloading

	Yes	No
All Libraries	0	100

Table #122: Percentage of libraries in the sample that have used any other service for E-book viewing or downloading

	Yes	No
All Libraries	9.09	90.91

Table #123: Percentage of libraries in the sample that have used any other service for E-book viewing or downloading, broken out by type of library

Type of Library	Yes	No
Public Library	0	100
College Library	15.38	84.62
Special Library	0	100

Table #124: Percentage of libraries in the sample that have used any other service for E-book viewing or downloading, broken out by college enrollment

College Enrollment	Yes	No
Below 7,000	28.57	71.43
7,001- 13,000	0	100
Above 13,000	0	100

Table #125: Percentage of libraries in the sample that have used any other service for E-book viewing or downloading, broken out for corporate and legal libraries

	Yes	No
Corporate	0	100
Legal	0	100

CHAPTER SIX: USE OF E-BOOK READER DEVICES

Percentage of Libraries that Lend Out an E-book Reader Device

A shade more than 13% of the libraries in the sample lend out to patrons some type of E-book reader device, the definition of which excludes CD-ROM, DVD and audio-only devices. Libraries at medium sized colleges appear the most likely to do so, although some public libraries are also dabbling in the lending out to patrons of E-book readers. However, many libraries are interested in acquiring and testing E-book readers, and 20% of the libraries in the sample have said that they will do just that in the next year.

Primary Research Group suspects that the library market is ripe for "E-book" seeding, similar to the seeding of k-12 academic institutions with Apple personal computers over the past ten years. Libraries are interested in E-books but do not quite know how to use them, catalog them, present them to patrons. Libraries do not have the manpower to do this work easily themselves; from the point of view of manufacturers of E-book reading devices, a lot can be gained in this market by providing instructional videos, easy to read and graphically illustrated how to instruction booklets (with emphasis on "easy" and "booklet".) Even modest point of purchase displays -- "Welcome to the world of E-books" -- "10,000" classics at your fingertips" "500 classic children's books for children aged 11-13". A small amount of focused marketing done by device and software manufacturers for the libraries could go a long way to promoting E-books usage in school, public and academic libraries.

Table #126: Percentage of libraries in the sample that lend out to patrons any type of E-book reader device designed specifically to access E-books (excluding CD-ROM readers)

	Yes	No
All Libraries	13.33	86.67

Table #127: Percentage of libraries in the sample that lend out to patrons any type of E-book reader device designed specifically to access E-books (excluding CD-ROM readers), broken out by type of library

Type of Library	Yes	No
College Library	13.33	86.67
Special Library	9.09	90.91

Table #128: Percentage of libraries in the sample that lend out to patrons any type of E-book reader device designed specifically to access E-books (excluding CD-ROM readers), broken out by college enrollment

College Enrollment	Yes	No
Below 7,000	9.09	90.91
7,001- 13,000	27.27	72.73
Above 13,000	0	100

Table #129: Percentage of libraries in the sample that lend out to patrons any type of E-book reader device designed specifically to access E-books (excluding CD-ROM readers), broken out for corporate and legal libraries

	Yes	No
Corporate	0	100
Legal	0	100

Table #130: Percentage of libraries in the sample that plan to purchase or test a type of E-book reader device designed specifically to access E-books, within the next year

	Yes	No
All Libraries	20.0	80.00

Table #131: Percentage of libraries in the sample that plan to purchase or test a type of E-book reader device designed specifically to access E-books, within the next year, broken out by type of library

Type of Library	Yes	No
College Library	13.79	86.21
Special Library	25.00	75.00

Table #132: Percentage of libraries in the sample that plan to purchase or test a type of E-book reader device designed specifically to access E-books, within the next year, broken out by college enrollment

College Enrollment	Yes	No
Below 7,000	10.00	90.00
7,001- 13,000	18.18	81.82
Above 13,000	0	100

Table #133: Percentage of libraries in the sample that plan to purchase or test a type of E-book reader device designed specifically to access E-books, within the next year, broken out for corporate and legal libraries

	Yes	No
Corporate	0	100
Legal	100	0

Table #134: Percentage of libraries in the sample that have used The Franklin E-bookman

	Yes	No
All Libraries	31.58	68.42

Table #135: Percentage of libraries in the sample that have used The Franklin E-bookman, broken out by type of library

Type of Library	Yes	No
Public Library	100	0
College Library	35.71	64.29
Special Library	16.67	83.33

Table #136: Percentage of libraries in the sample that have used The Franklin E-bookman, broken out by college enrollment

College Enrollment	Yes	No
Below 7,000	33.33	66.67
7,001- 13,000	36.36	63.64
Above 13,000	33.33	66.67

Table #137: Percentage of libraries in the sample that have used The Franklin E-bookman, broken out for corporate and legal libraries

	Yes	No
Corporate	0	100
Legal	0	100

Table #138: Percentage of libraries in the sample that have used Rocket E-book or Softbook Reader

	Yes	No
All Libraries	14.04	85.96

Table #139: Percentage of libraries in the sample that have used Rocket E-book or Softbook Reader, broken out by type of library

Type of Library	Yes	No
College Library	25.00	75.00
Special Library	4.17	95.83

Table #140: Percentage of libraries in the sample that have used Rocket E-book or Softbook Reader, broken out by college enrollment

College Enrollment	Yes	No
Below 7,000	44.44	55.56
7,001- 13,000	9.09	90.91
Above 13,000	33.33	66.67

Table #141: Percentage of libraries in the sample that have used Rocket E-book or Softbook Reader, broken out for corporate and legal libraries

	Yes	No
Corporate	0	100
Legal	0	100

Table #142: Percentage of libraries in the sample that have used RCA REB 1100

	Yes	No
All Libraries	17.54	82.46

Table #143: Percentage of libraries in the sample that have used RCA REB 1100, broken out by type of library

Type of Library	Yes	No
College Library	21.43	78.57
Special Library	8.33	91.67

Table #144: Percentage of libraries in the sample that have used RCA REB 1100, broken out by college enrollment

College Enrollment	Yes	No
Below 7,000	44.44	55.56
7,001- 13,000	9.09	90.91
Above 13,000	16.67	83.33

Table #145: Percentage of libraries in the sample that have used RCA REB 1100, broken out for corporate and legal libraries

	Yes	No
Corporate	12.50	87.50
Legal	0	100

Table #146: Percentage of libraries in the sample that have used GO READER

	Yes	No
All Libraries	1.75	98.25

Table #147: Percentage of libraries in the sample that have used GO READER, broken out by type of library

Type of Library	Yes	No
College Library	3.57	96.43
Special Library	0	100

Table #148: Percentage of libraries in the sample that have used GO READER, broken out by college enrollment

College Enrollment	Yes	No
Below 7,000	0	100
7,001- 13,000	9.09	90.91
Above 13,000	0	100

Table #149: Percentage of libraries in the sample that have used GO READER, broken out for corporate and legal libraries

	Yes	No
Corporate	0	100
Legal	0	100

Table #150: Percentage of libraries in the sample that have used Palm Pilot/ Peanut Press

	Yes	No
All Libraries	28.07	71.93

Table #151: Percentage of libraries in the sample that have used Palm Pilot/ Peanut Press, broken out by type of library

Type of Library	Yes	No
College Library	32.14	67.86
Special Library	25.00	75.00

Table #152: Percentage of libraries in the sample that have used Palm Pilot/ Peanut Press, broken out by college enrollment

College Enrollment	Yes	No
Below 7,000	22.22	77.78
7,001- 13,000	45.45	54.55
Above 13,000	33.33	66.67

Table #153: Percentage of libraries in the sample that have used Palm Pilot/ Peanut Press, broken out for corporate and legal libraries

	Yes	No
Corporate	37.50	62.50
Legal	16.67	83.33

Table #154: Percentage of libraries in the sample that have used Adobe Acrobat E-book Reader

	Yes	No
All Libraries	59.65	40.35

Table #155: Percentage of libraries in the sample that have used Adobe Acrobat E-book Reader, broken out for corporate and legal libraries

	Yes	No
Corporate	75.00	25.00
Legal	100	0

Table #156: Percentage of libraries in the sample that have used Adobe Acrobat E-book Reader, broken out by type of library

Type of Library	Yes	No
Public Library	33.33	66.67
College Library	42.86	57.14
Special Library	83.33	16.67

Table #157: Percentage of libraries in the sample that have used Adobe Acrobat E-book Reader, broken out by college enrollment

College Enrollment	Yes	No
Below 7,000	22.22	77.78
7,001- 13,000	63.64	36.36
Above 13,000	33.33	66.67

Table #158: Percentage of libraries in the sample that have used Adobe Acrobat E-book Reader, broken out for corporate and legal libraries

Type of Library	Yes	No
Corporate	75	25
Legal	100	0

Table #159: Percentage of libraries in the sample that have used Microsoft Reader Software

	Yes	No
All Libraries	33.33	66.67

Table #160: Percentage of libraries in the sample that have used Microsoft Reader Software, broken out by type of library

Type of Library	Yes	No
College Library	32.14	67.86
Special Library	33.33	66.67

Table #161: Percentage of libraries in the sample that have used Microsoft Reader Software, broken out by college enrollment

College Enrollment	Yes	No
Below 7,000	33.33	66.67
7,001- 13,000	36.36	63.64
Above 13,000	33.33	66.67

Table #162: Percentage of libraries in the sample that have used Microsoft Reader Software, broken out for corporate and legal libraries

	Yes	No
Corporate	25.00	75.00
Legal	33.33	66.67

CHAPTER SEVEN: LIBRARY USE OF PUBLIC DOMAIN E-BOOKS

Use of public domain E-books have become increasingly popular, and services that offer public domain E-books are functioning as a kind of "trojan horse" for commercial E-books, spreading the E-book concept and accustoming library patrons to their use. It may be possible for commercial publishers to "piggy-back" on public domain E-books by offering aspects of their collections at very low prices that entice libraries. Low price offerings encourage end user libraries to familiarize themselves with other aspects of a publisher's collection and, in general, become ancillary revenues for publishers while providing an extensive, easy to search but low priced reference source for researchers.

More than two thirds of the libraries in the sample offer access to public domain E-book collections. It is our regret at Primary Research Group that we did not include in this study more questions about how exactly these collections are being used, since they may be pre-cursors to more extensive use of E-books in the commercial arena that dominates information usage at college, research and special libraries.

For the most part, the public domain collections are used much more extensively by academic and public libraries. The public domain collections are often composed largely of classics for which the original copyright protection period has expired. The three major public access E-book collections are: Project Gutenberg, Bartleby.com and E-Text.Lib. Project Gutenberg was the most commonly used service, followed by Bartleby.com and E-text.lib.

Table #163: Percentage of libraries in the sample that offer patron access to any public domain E-books

	Yes	No
All Libraries	67.86	32.14

Table #164: Percentage of libraries in the sample that offer patron access to any public domain E-books, broken out by type of library

Type of Library	Yes	No
College Library	68.75	31.25
Special Library	50.00	50.00

All three public libraries in the sample offered access to public domain E-books.

Table #165: Percentage of libraries in the sample that offer patron access to any public domain E-books, broken out by college enrollment

College Enrollment	Yes	No
Below 7,000	71.43	28.57
7,001- 13,000	57.14	42.86
Above 13,000	100	0

Table #166: Percentage of libraries in the sample that offer patron access to any public domain E-books, broken out for corporate and legal libraries

	Yes	No
Corporate	0	100
Legal	0	100

Table #167: Percentage of libraries in the sample that plan to offer patron access to any public domain E-books within the next year

	Yes	No
All Libraries	69.77	30.23

Table #168: Percentage of libraries in the sample that plan to offer patron access to any public domain E-books within the next year, broken out by type of library

Type of Library	Yes	No
College Library	72.41	27.59
Special Library	50.00	50.00

Table #169: Percentage of libraries in the sample that plan to offer patron access to any public domain E-books within the next year, broken out by college enrollment

College Enrollment	Yes	No
Below 7,000	55.56	44.44
7,001- 13,000	72.73	27.27
Above 13,000	85.71	14.29

Table #170: Percentage of libraries in the sample that plan to offer patron access to any public domain E-books within the next year, broken out by college enrollment

	Yes	No
Corporate	0	100
Legal	0	100

Table #171: Percentage of libraries in the sample that offer access or have used Project Gutenberg

	Yes	No
All Libraries	91.18	8.82

Table #172: Percentage of libraries in the sample that offer access or have used Project Gutenberg, broken out by type of library

Type of Library	Yes	No
College Library	87.50	12.50
Special Library	100	0

Table #173: Percentage of libraries in the sample that offer access or have used Project Gutenberg, broken out by college enrollment

College Enrollment	Yes	No
Below 7,000	87.50	12.50
7,001- 13,000	77.78	22.22
Above 13,000	100	0

Table #174: Percentage of libraries in the sample that offer access or have used Project Gutenberg, broken out for corporate and legal libraries

	Yes	No
Corporate	0	100
Legal	0	100

Table #175: Percentage of libraries in the sample that offer access or have used Bartleby.com

	Yes	No
All Libraries	23.53	76.47

Table #176: Percentage of libraries in the sample that offer access or have used Bartleby.com, broken out by type of library

Type of Library	Yes	No
College Library	20.83	79.17
Special Library	16.67	83.33

Table #177: Percentage of libraries in the sample that offer access or have used Bartleby.com, broken out by college enrollment

College Enrollment	Yes	No
Below 7,000	25.00	75.00
7,001- 13,000	22.22	77.78
Above 13,000	20.00	80.00

Table #178: Percentage of libraries in the sample that offer access or have used Etext.Lib (College of Virginia)

	Yes	No
All Libraries	11.76	88.24

Table #179: Percentage of libraries in the sample that offer access or have used Etext.Lib (College of Virginia), broken out by type of library

Type of Library	Yes	No
College Library	12.50	87.50
Special Library	16.67	83.33

Table #180: Percentage of libraries in the sample that offer access or have used Etext.Lib (College of Virginia), broken out by college enrollment

College Enrollment	Yes	No
Below 7,000	12.50	87.50
7,001- 13,000	22.22	77.78
Above 13,000	0	100

Table #181: Percentage of libraries in the sample that offer access or have used any other public access E-book collections

	Yes	No
All Libraries	5.88	94.12

Table #182: Percentage of libraries in the sample that offer access or have used any other public access E-book collections, broken out by type of library

Type of Library	Yes	No
College Library	4.17	95.83
Special Library	0	100

Table #183: Percentage of libraries in the sample that offer access or have used any other public access E-book collections, broken out by college enrollment

College Enrollment	Yes	No
Below 7,000	12.50	87.50
7,001- 13,000	0	100
Above 13,000	0	100

CHAPTER EIGHT: RANKING LIBRARY REASONS FOR USING E-BOOKS

Two reasons for using E-books stood out from all the others. Those reasons were: E-books can be accessed "around the clock" and E-books can potentially be accessed by more than one individual at a time. All other reasons for using E-books, their potentially lower costs, resistance to physical damage, low storage costs, volume discounts for E-book purchases or even their "searchability" were deemed less important by librarians interviewed.

The results suggest that librarians view E-books as particularly important vehicles for "high use" items that are constantly needed, at all hours, sometimes in "small doses" and often by more than one individual at a time. The key problem is: how to provide E-book versions of these key, frequently cited works in such a way that publisher revenues are expanded in a cost attractive way to libraries? The gain to library patrons has to be: reduced time in waiting to obtain high use items and reduced pressure to return these items quickly. The gain to publishers should be: lower printing and fulfillment costs and greater revenues than they would have had supplying exclusively print versions of the same work.

Table #183: Ranking reasons for E-book usage: no damaged copies returned

	Important reason for using E-books in libraries	Moderately important reason for using E-books in libraries	indifferent
All Libraries	47.37	34.21	18.42

Table 184#: Ranking reasons for E-book usage: no damaged copies returned, broken out by type of library

Type of Library	Important reason for using E-books in libraries	Moderately important reason for using E-books in libraries	Indifferent
Public Library	33.33	66.67	0
College Library	42.31	34.62	23.08
Special Library	62.50	25.00	12.50

Table #185 Ranking reasons for E-book usage: no damaged copies returned, broken out by college enrollment

College Enrollment	Important reason for using E-books in libraries	Moderately important reason for using E-books in libraries	Indifferent
Below 7,000	25.00	37.50	37.50
7,001-13,000	45.45	36.36	18.18
Above 13,000	60.00	40.00	0

Table #186: Ranking reasons for E-book usage: books can be taken out 24 hours per day

	Important reason for using E-books in libraries	Moderately important reason for using E-books in libraries	indifferent
All Libraries	50.00	26.32	23.68

Table #187: Ranking reasons for E-book usage: books can be taken out 24 hours per day, broken out by type of library

Type of Library	Important reason for using E-books in libraries	Moderately important reason for using E-books in libraries	Indifferent
Public Library	66.67	0	33.33
College Library	50.00	30.77	19.23
Special Library	50.00	12.50	37.50

Table #188: ranking reasons for E-book usage: books can be taken out 24 hours per day, broken out by college enrollment

College Enrollment	Important reason for using E-books in libraries	Moderately important reason for using E-books in libraries	Indifferent
Below 7,000	62.50	25.00	12.50
7,001-13,000	45.45	27.27	27.27
Above 13,000	60.00	40.00	0

Table #189: Ranking reasons for E-book usage: books can be searched with keywords or other search tools

	Important reason for using E-books in libraries reason	Moderately important reason for using E-books in libraries	Indifference
All Libraries	46.15	33.33	20.51

Table #190: Ranking reasons for E-book usage: books can be searched with keywords or other search tools, broken out by type of library

Type of Library	Important reason for using E-books in libraries	Moderately important reason for using E-books in libraries	Indifferent
Public Library	66.67	33.33	0
College Library	53.85	30.77	15.38
Special Library	22.22	44.44	33.33

Table #191: ranking reasons for E-books usage: books can be searched with keywords or other search tools, broken out by college enrollment

College Enrollment	Important reason for using E-books in libraries	Moderately important reason for using E-books in libraries	Indifferent
Below 7,000	75.00	12.50	12.50
7,001-13,000	54.55	36.36	9.09
Above 13,000	20.00	60.00	20.00

Table #192: Ranking reasons for E-book usage: books can be updated quickly via the internet

	Important reason for using E-books in libraries reason	Moderately important reason for using E-books in libraries	Indifference
All Libraries	43.59	30.77	25.64

Table #193: Ranking reasons for E-book usage: books can be updated quickly via the internet, broken out by type of library

Type of Library	Important reason for using E-books in libraries	Moderately important reason for using E-books in libraries	Indifferent
Public Library	0	66.67	33.33
College Library	46.15	26.92	26.92
Special Library	44.44	33.33	22.22

Table #194: ranking reasons for E-book usage: books can be updated quickly via the internet, broken out by college enrollment

College Enrollment	Important reason for using E-books in libraries	Moderately important reason for using E-books in libraries	Indifferent
Below 7,000	50.00	37.50	12.50
7,001-13,000	45.45	27.27	27.27
Above 13,000	40.00	20.00	40.00

Table #195: Ranking reasons for E-book usage: E-books require no shelf space and will lower costs

	Important reason for using E-books in libraries reason	Moderately important reason for using E-books in libraries	Indifference
All Libraries	37.50	25.00	37.50

Table #196: Ranking reasons for E-book usage: E-books require no shelf space and will lower costs, broken out by type of library

Type of Library	Important reason for using E-books in libraries	Moderately important reason for using E-books in libraries	Indifferent
Public Library	33.33	33.33	33.33
College Library	37.04	29.63	33.33
Special Library	33.33	11.11	55.56

Table #197: ranking reasons for E-book usage: E-books require no shelf space and will lower costs, broken out by college enrollment

College Enrollment	Important reason for using E-books in libraries	Moderately important reason for using E-books in libraries	Indifferent
Below 7,000	37.50	25.00	37.50
7,001-13,000	27.27	27.27	45.45
Above 13,000	66.67	33.33	0

Table #198: Ranking reasons for E-book usage: volume discounts for E-book purchases

	Important reason for using E-books in libraries reason	Moderately important reason for using E-books in libraries	Indifference
All Libraries	34.21	31.58	34.21

Table #199: Ranking reasons for E-book usage: volume discounts for E-book purchases, broken out by type of library

Type of Library	Important reason for using E-books in libraries	Moderately important reason for using E-books in libraries	Indifferent
Public Library	33.33	33.33	33.33
College Library	38.46	30.77	30.77
Special Library	25.00	25.00	50.00

Table #200: ranking reasons for E-book usage: volume discounts for E-book purchases, broken out by college enrollment

College Enrollment	Important reason for using E-books in libraries	Moderately important reason for using E-books in libraries	Indifferent
Below 7,000	37.50	25.00	37.50
7,001-13,000	36.36	36.36	27.27
Above 13,000	60.00	40.00	0

Table #201: Ranking reasons for E-book usage: deal allows multiple access so that more readers can view materials

	Important reason for using E-books in libraries	Moderately important reason for using E-books in libraries	Indifference
All Libraries	58.97	23.08	17.95

Table #202: Ranking reasons for E-book usage: deal allows multiple access so that more readers can view materials, broken out by type of library

Type of Library	Important reason for using E-books in libraries	Moderately important reason for using E-books in libraries	Indifferent
Public Library	66.67	33.33	0
College Library	55.56	22.22	22.22
Special Library	62.50	25.00	12.50

Table #203: ranking reasons for E-book usage: deal allows multiple access so that more readers can view materials, broken out by college enrollment

College Enrollment	Important reason for using E-books in libraries	Moderately important reason for using E-books in libraries	Indifferent
Below 7,000	50.00	25.00	25.00
7,001-13,000	72.73	9.09	18.18
Above 13,000	33.33	50.00	16.67

CHAPTER NINE: MOST COMMONLY USED TYPES OF E-BOOKS

Reference and professional and technical literature dominated the selection of subject categories of E-books that attracted the most interest among librarians. A third leading field was educational materials other than textbooks, reflecting the growing use of the internet to post supplementary educational materials in traditional college classes, and the growing popularity of distance education.

Table #205: Subject Categories of E-books that attract the most interest among library patrons

	Reference	Fiction	Technical & Professional Literature	Textbooks	Other Education Materials	Other
All Libraries	44.74	5.26	31.58	2.63	13.16	2.63

Table #206: Subject Categories of E-books that attract the most interest among library patrons, broken out by type of library

Type of Library	Reference	Fiction	Technical & Professional Literature	Textbooks	Other Education Materials	Other
Public Library	0	33.33	66.67	0	0	0
College Library	50.00	3.85	26.92	3.85	11.54	3.85
Special Library	50.00	0	25.00	0	25.00	0

Table #207: subject categories of E-books that attract the most interest among library patrons, broken out by college enrollment

College Enrollment	Reference	Fiction	Technical & Professional Literature	Textbooks	Other education materials	Other
Below 7,000	71.43	0	0	0	14.29	14.29
7,001-13,000	45.45	0	36.36	9.09	9.09	0
Above 13,000	33.33	16.67	33.33	0	16.67	0

Table #208: Percentage of libraries in the sample that allow access to their E-book collection from non-library locations

	Yes	No
All Libraries	82.05	17.95

Table #209: Percentage of libraries in the sample that allow access to their E-book collection from non-library locations, broken out by type of library

Type of Library	Yes	No
College Library	85.71	14.29
Special Library	71.43	28.57

Table #210: Percentage of libraries in the sample that allow access to their E-book collection for non-library locations, broken out by college enrollment

College Enrollment	Yes	No
Below 7,000	87.50	12.50
7,001- 13,000	83.33	16.67
Above 13,000	83.33	16.67

CHAPTER TEN: DATA FROM A SECOND SAMPLE EXCLUSIVELY OF CORPORATE LIBRARIES

Our initial sample of 80 libraries had only eight corporate libraries, so to get a better view of this sector we included two questions about E-books to a sample of corporate and other business libraries that were being interviewed in connection with our 2002-2003 edition of Corporate Library Benchmarks. Forty-eight corporate libraries returned data from a mail questionnaire or answered a phone query in time to be included in this report. The complete data set from the full sample of 70 corporate and other business libraries is included in our study *Corporate Library Benchmarks, 2002-03 edition.*

Most of the companies in this second sample were major corporations, consulting firms or the business libraries of trade associations or college MBA programs. This sample is dominated by major companies.

4 of 44 corporate libraries sampled (that could answer this question) noted that they planned to add an additional book site license from a publisher that they had not had a license with previously.

15 of the 47 corporate or other business libraries sampled spent anything at all on E-books. Mean spending on E-books for all corporate libraries in the second sample, including those that did not use E-books or spend anything at all on E-books, was $9, 957, with a median of 0. The verbatim list of the spending totals of the fifteen libraries in the sample that spent anything at all on E-books is reproduced below:

Table #211: Annual Spending for E-books by Corporate/Business Libraries in the Second Sample

Type of Company	E-book Spending, 2002
Major Insurance Company	$42,000
Major Defense Contractor	$180,000
Medium-Sized Bank	$10,000
Pharmaceutical Company	$5,000
Trade Association	$10,000
Publication Library	$29,000
MBA Program Library	$40,000
MBA Program Library	$24,000
MBA Program Library	$15,000
Scientific Consulting Firm Library	$18,000
Research-Oriented Consulting Firm Library	$30,000
Non-Profit	$1,000
Major Telecom Equipment Manufacturer Library	$26,000
Research Company Library	$25,000
Major Pharmaceutical Company Library	$16,000

27% of the libraries in the second corporate sample had a site license for electronic versions of professional books, and 42% had site licenses for reference books or directories, though these figures also include free access to electronic versions linked to the purchase of print versions. Some librarians may also have included CD-ROM site licenses to popular directories.

CHAPTER ELEVEN: USE OF E-BOOKS BY DISTANCE LEARNING PROGRAMS AND ELECTRONIC COURSE RESERVE SERVICES

Two other areas of growing E-book demand are distance learning programs, and the electronic reserve services of academic libraries. In order to better understand growing E-book demand in these two sectors, we've included data on both of these sectors from two recent studies, *The Survey of Academic Libraries, 2002 Edition* (June 2002) and *The Survey of Distance and Cyberlearning Programs in Higher Education, 2002 Edition* (July 2002). The sampling for both of these studies was done largely in the second quarter of 2002.

About 34% of libraries offer an electronic reserve service to support training, course work, or other organizational objectives.

Table #212: Percentage of libraries that offer an electronic reserve service to support training, course work, or any other organizational objectives

	Yes	No
All libraries	33.93	66.07

Table #213: Percentage of libraries that offer an electronic reserve service to support training, course work, or any other organizational objectives, broken out by Carnegie classification

Carnegie Classification	Yes	No
Associates of Arts	17.65	82.35
Baccalaureate	26.32	73.68
Doctoral	40	60
Masters	70	30

Table #214: Percentage of libraries that offer an electronic reserve service to support training, course work, or any other organizational objectives, broken out by the size of the library based on the level of expenditures

Size Class	Yes	No
Quartile I	26.67	73.33
Quartile II	23.53	76.47
Quartile III	50	50
Quartile IV	38.46	61.54

Mean Spending On The Start-Up Of The Electronic Reserve Services

Libraries reported spending a mean of $4,500 to start-up electronic reserve services.

Table #215: Mean spending in U.S. dollars on the start-up of the electronic reserves services

	Mean	Median	Minimum	Maximum
All libraries	4,500	4,500	0	15,000

Table #216: Mean spending in U.S. dollars on the start-up of the electronic reserves services, broken out by Carnegie classification

Carnegie Classification	Mean	Median	Minimum	Maximum
Associates of Arts	500	500	0	1,000
Baccalaureate	5,250	5,000	4,000	7,000
Doctoral	1,000	1,000	1,000	1,000
Engineering	0	0	0	0
Masters	11,000	11,000	7,000	15,000

Table #217:   Mean spending in U.S. dollars on the start-up of the electronic reserves services, broken out by the size of the library based on the level of expenditures

Size Class	Mean	Median	Minimum	Maximum
Quartile I	6,000	6,000	5,000	7,000
Quartile II	3,000	4,000	0	5,000
Quartile III	500	500	0	1,000
Quartile IV	4,000	4,000	1,000	7,000

16.67% of the colleges in the sample note that they currently make significant use of E-books in their cirriculum. E-book usage seemed unrelated to program size or type, though doctoral-level colleges in the sample used them more than other types of colleges.

Table #218:   Percentage of Distance Learning Programs that make Significant Use of E-books in Curriculum

	Yes	No
All colleges	**16.67**	**83.33**

Table #219:   Percentage of Distance Learning Programs that make Significant Use of E-books in Curriculum, Broken Out by Carnegie Class

Carnegie classification	Yes	No
Associates	21.43	78.57
Baccalaureate	14.29	85.71
Business	0.00	100.00
Doctoral	40.00	60.00
Masters	14.29	85.71
Research	0.00	100.00
Theology	0.00	100.00

Table #220: Percentage of Distance Learning Programs that make Significant Use of E-books in Curriculum, Broken Out by the Size of the Distance Learning Program

Number of Distance Learning Enrollment	Yes	No
200 or less	29.41	70.59
200-400	5.88	94.12
400-1000	12.50	87.50
1,000-more	23.08	76.92

Far more programs noted that their distance learning students spent more on education materials than their counterparts in traditional classes. While the clear majority of program directors (57.14%) felt that their distance learning students spent about the same amount as students in traditional classes, far more (36.51%) said that the distance learning students spent more, than said that students in traditional classes spent more. Only a shade more than 6% of the distance learning program directors interviewed felt that distance learning students spent less on educational materials than their counterparts in traditional classes. Directors of the larger distance learning programs had a somewhat greater tendency to believe that distance learning students spent more than

Table #221: Spending for Educational Materials by Distance Learning Students Contrasted with Such Spending for Traditional Classes

	Greater than	Less than	About the same
All colleges	36.51	6.35	57.14

Table #222: Spending for Educational Materials by Distance Learning Students Contrasted with Such Spending for Traditional Classes, Broken Out by Carnegie Class

Carnegie classification	Greater than	Less than	About the same
Associates	30.77	3.85	65.38
Baccalaureate	57.14	14.29	28.57
Business	33.33	0.00	66.67
Doctoral	60.00	20.00	20.00
Masters	33.33	6.67	60.00
Research	33.33	0.00	66.67
Theology	0.00	0.00	100.00

Table #223: Spending for Educational Materials by Distance Learning Students Contrasted with Such Spending for Traditional Classes, Broken Out by the Size of the Distance Learning Program

Number of Distance Learning Enrollment	Greater than	Less than	About the same
200 or less	25.00	12.50	62.50
200-400	29.41	11.76	58.82
400-1000	56.25	0.00	43.75
1,000-more	35.71	0.00	64.29

Table #224: Percentage of Course Materials Used by Distance Learning Students that is Designed Specifically for Distance Learning Courses, Broken Out by Total Enrollment of the College

Total Enrollment of College	Yes	No
Less than 2,000	52	48
2,000-4,000	36.71	63.29
4,000-8,000	49.6	50.4
More than 8000	44.8	55.20

Table #225: Percentage of Course Materials Used by Distance Learning Students that is Designed Specifically for Traditional Classes, Broken Out by the Size of the Distance Learning Program

Number of Distance Learning Enrollment	Yes	No
200 or less	54.3	45.7
200-400	60	40
400-1000	58.75	41.25
1,000-more	47.20	52.80

Table #226: Percentage of Course Materials Used by Distance Learning Students that is Designed Specifically for Traditional Classes, Broken Out by Total Enrollment of the College

Total Enrollment of College	Yes	No
Less than 2,000	48	52
2,000-4,000	63.29	36.71
4,000-8,000	50.4	49.6
More than 8000	55.20	44.8

SELECT STUDY PARTICIPANTS: FIRST SAMPLE

A.O. Smith Corporation
Ablilene Christian College
Alabama State College
Algohaquin Public Libray
Alice Lloyd College
Allentown State Hospital Library
Arizona Transportation Research Center
Baltimore City Community College
Beloit College Library
Berlin Memorial Hospital-Medical Library
Bohnert LIbraria Georgia Power Co.
Bowling Green State College
Bridgewater State College
Carl Sandburg College
Casselsbrock & Blackwell
Citrus College
Cleveland State College
Clinch Valley College of the College of Virginia
Colby-Sawyer College
Conemough Memorial medical center
Conseco Direct
Eastern Washington College
Faulkner College - Nichols Library
Hardin Simmons
Houston Public Library

APPENDIX 1: THE QUESTIONNAIRE

DEFINITIONS:

The term E-books include: print on demand books, intranet licenses for books, content for electronic book readers devices, downloads of books from websites, and services that allow the library to view books on a server. For the purposes of this survey, the term E-books excludes books on CD-ROM. Note: even if the library does not use E-books, it is important for our random sample that you answer the questions. The results are projected to a general population of American libraries.

NetLibrary

1) Does the library have a current subscription to NetLibrary or its successor service?*
____Yes   ____No

2) How much did the library spend for its NetLibrary subscription in the past year? $_____

3) Have you ever heard of the company NetLibrary?
____Yes   ____No

Electronic Book Licenses with Specific Publishers

1) Does the library have a subscription to any other E-book service or a deal with any specific publishers? (please include intranet licensing deals with BOOK publishers)
____Yes   ____No

2) If so, with which publishers or services has the library concluded deals:

_____
_____
_____
_____
_____
_____

3) If the library has deals with specific publishers for electronic access to books, about how much do you estimate that the library spent on such deals in the past year?
$_____

4) How much do you estimate that the library will spend on E-books (including intranet licenses with book publishers) in the coming year? $_____

5) Is the library considering the purchase of an E-book or intranet license with any particular book publishers or service in the upcoming two years with which it currently does not have a deal?

____Yes   ____No

6) If so, which publishers or vendors is the library considering?

_____
_____
_____
_____

Sources of Funding for E-books

1) If the library currently spends anything on E-books, does the

funding come out of the traditional book budget?

___Yes   ___No   ___Not Applicable

2) Has the library ever received special funding to develop E-books?

___Yes   ___No

3)Do you think that the library may be able to obtain such funding in the future if the E-book market develops quickly?

___Yes   ___No

Preferences for Specific Forms of E-books

1) If the library has an E-book collection, is it housed on the library's own servers or intranet, or on the remote server or web page of the publisher, or does the library have both of these types of arrangements?

a) housed on own server or intranet b) housed on remote server   c) both of these arrangements

2) Has the library ever ordered custom books or particular chapters or sections of books from a print-on-demand publisher? (Note: this type of publisher holds reserves of content connected to fast printers and prints out book segments, chapter, and entire books and sometimes aggregates them into compendiums or collections -- all on demand)

___Yes, library has made such orders ___No, library has not made such orders

3) Please assign a rank 1,2,3,4,5 to assess the library's interest in each of the 5 major types of E-book technology presented below. Assign #1 to the option that most interests the library, and 5 to the option that least interests the library. Assign one rank to each option; do not assign the same number twice.

a) E-books downloaded from web site_____ ;   b) print on demand _____ ;
c) books accessed through E-book-reader _____ ;   d) intranet licensed E-books _____ ; e) E-books accessed from web site but not downloaded_____.

Impact of E-books on Traditional Book Collections

1) How would you say that the library E-book collection has impacted print book collection development:

a) we have substituted E-books for print books and reduced print book purchases
b) E-books have stimulated demand for print books and led us to purchase more print books
c) E-books have had not real impact on our print book collection development

2) for the most part, do your E-book collection deals enable the end user to:

a) download a digital copy of the book
b) print out a print version of the entire book
c) print out only selected pages from the book
d) read only, with no downloading or printing

3) Does the library formally monitor and have statistical data on the use of E-books?

____Yes   ____No

4) Do most of your E-book licenses allow for any simultaneous use of titles in the E-book collection?

____Yes   ____No

Use of Specific E-book Web Sites, Software or Devices

1) To your knowledge, has the library used any of the following services for E-book viewing or downloading. Exclude use of these services for traditional print books or traditional cassette audiobooks. Check all those that the library has ever used for E-books or electronically delivered audiobooks.

a)E-books.com ____
b)Teach now____
c) Audiobooks.com____
d) Lightning Source____
e) Amazon.Com____
f) Overdrive.Com____
g)1st Books.Com____
h) 00H00.com____
i) Ebrary____
j) Mightywords.com (fatbrain)____

k) Librius.Com____
l) Books 24X7____
m) lbooks.com____
n) Adobe E-bookstore____
o) BarnesandNoble.com____
p) Pocketmanager.com____
t) Other: Please specify:_____
____

E-book Reader Devices

1) Does the library lend out to patron any type of E-book reader device designed specifically to access E-books? (Exclude CD-ROM readers)
____Yes   ____No

2) Does the library plan to purchase or test any such device within the next year?

____Yes   ____No

3) Has the library used any of the following devices or software: (please check all that apply)

The Franlkin E-bookman ____
Rocket E-book or Softbook Reader ____
RCA REB 1100 ____
GO READER   ____
Palm Pilot/ Peanut Press   ____
Adobe Acrobat E-book Reader____
Microsoft Reader Software ____

Use of Public Domain E-books

1) Does the library offer patrons access to any public domain E-books?

2) Does the library plan to offer access to any public domain E-books within the next year?

____Yes   ____No

3) Does the library offer access or has the library used any of the following public access E-book collections: (check all that apply)

a)Project Gutenberg____
b)Bartleby.Com____
c)Etext.Lib (College of Virginia)____
d) other. (please specify)

_____
_____

Evaluation of E-book Usage by Patrons & Staff

1) Evaluate the following Reasons for choosing electronic books by assigning each reason a 1, 2 or 3 with 1 signifying an important reason for purchasing E-books and 3 signifying indifference.

1) No damaged copies returned____
2) Books can be taken our 24 hours per day____
3) Books can be searched with keywords or other search tools____
4) Books can be updated quickly via the internet____
5) E-books require no shelf space and will lower costs ____
6) Volume discounts for E-book purchases____
7) deal allows multiple access so that more readers can view materials____

2) What kind of E-books attract the most interest from your library patrons (choose one)

1) reference titles
2) fiction
3) technical & professional literature
4) textbooks
5) training manuals, computer training guides and
          other educational materials
6) Other (please specify)_____
__

3) Does the library allow access to its E-book collection from non-library locations?

____Yes   ____No

Survey of College Marketing Programs
Publcation Date: 2002
Price: $244.50

This landmark study of college marketing practices imparts critical benchmarking data now broken out by Carnegie Class for even better benchmarking performance. Hundreds of Table #s of data and commentary describe how American colleges and universities market themselves to prospective students. 92 American colleges and universities participated, including: 11 major research universities 22 baccalaureate-level colleges, 21 masters-granting colleges, 4 - theology institutes, and 25 community or junior colleges. Covers traditional marketing, internet marketing, a much more.

SURVEY OF ADULT & CONTINUING EDUCATION PROGRAMS IN HIGHER EDUCATION
Special Discount Price: $139.00 (set of two volumes) if ordered before September 15, 2002   Publication Date: October 1999

The Survey of Adult & Continuing Education Programs in Higher Education presents the findings of a detailed survey of college adult and continuing education programs, focusing on their revenues and expenditures, advertising and marketing practices, technology use practices, course offerings, student demographics, and other aspects of continuing & adult education program management.

DIGITAL CONTENT MARKETS FOR PUBLISHERS OF BOOKS, MAGAZINES, RESEARCH REPORTS, NEWSPAPERS, JOURNALS, NEWSLETTERS, & DIRECTORIES
Price: $1695.00   Publication Date: January, 2002

This special report from Primary Research Group is based on more than 500 interviews with publishers, aggregators, and information end users. The report presents detailed data on the overall market for text-based digital content, and breaks out the market by segment for publishers of books, newsletters, trade magazines, consumer magazines, journals, research reports, newspapers, directories and mailing lists. The report also looks at certain institutional and subject areas such as publishing by colleges, publishing by trade associations, and medical and legal publishing. Data in the report is based on 300 interviews with North American publishing companies and distributors, as well as 200 interviews with end users in corporations and libraries. For each type of publication, and for selected areas of publishing defined by the subject matter or type of parent institution, the report presents data on: 1) current and planned use of digital

storefronts and other types of web content distribution, 2) spending to build digital distribution infrastructure, 3) use of third party syndicators such as QPASS and Isyndicate, 4) distribution through major commercial online services, 5) use of html, Microsoft Word, pdf and Asci, 6) current or planned use of encryption technology, 7) % of total content sales through digital sales, 8) % of ad revenues through online sources, 9) % of new order for print products through web site, 10) assessment of impact of digital publishing on print revenues, 11) % of print content available on the web, 12) % of digital content available in print format, 13) plans to make available print content on the web, 14) availability of content in CD-ROM, 15) comparison of CD-ROM to web distribution revenues, 16) web site development costs, 17) web site hosting costs
18) Frequency of editing the web site, 19) web site outsourcing policies and other factors in digital publishing.

US Corporate Markets for Distance Learning & Online Training
Special Discount Price for Colleges & Universities:
Price: $1895 Special price for (accredited colleges only): $1195.00
Publication Date: March 2001

This special report, sold to industry for almost $2,000.00, presents the results of a survey of more than 400 U.S. companies. The report breaks out the use of distance learning by type of industry, company size and other variables useful to marketers of online training. The report is designed to help vendors to quickly ascertain levels of current and future demand for online training and distance learning courses. Survey data is supplemented by with secondary data from SEC filings, government and trade association sources and other secondary sources to provide a complete overview of corporate markets for distance learning in the USA.

CREATING THE DIGITAL LIBRARY
Publication Date: April 2000   Price: $75.00   isbn#: 1-57440-047-9

This report profiles the efforts of major American and Canadian corporate, academic, legal, medical, public and other libraries to digitize their collections and otherwise develop and distribute digital content. Compare your libraries efforts to those of some of North America's most prominent libraries. Includes coverage of copyright issues, technical issues, negotiations with publishers and electronic information services, and other issues relevent to the development of the digital library. Written by Cheryl Knott Malone, Assistant Professor of Library Science at the Graduate School of Library & Information Science, the College of Illinois at Urbana., and James Moses, President of Primary Research Group.

COPYRIGHT INFORMATION PURCHASING AND USAGE: BEST PRACTICES OF AMERICAN CORPORATIONS

Publication Date: October 2001   Price: $295.00

Based on interviews with more than a dozen major American corporations and government agencies, and including detailed profiles of FORD MOTOR COMPANY, THE US DEPARTMENT OF STATE, COMPAQ, MICROSOFT, LUCENT TECHNOLOGIES, AAB, and other companies and agencies.